Flotsam & Jetsam

A half-life of poems

Lana Hunneyball

For all the Wild at Heart
who've met the fragile flame,
pass through it
and feel the spaces as their very soul.

Contents

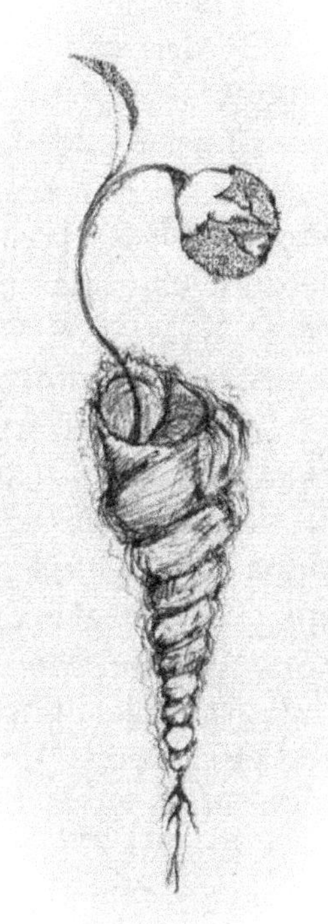

"Life is giving birth to yourself."

Modernised from
Erich Fromm

Preface

You are invited on a journey—twenty years of flotsam and jetsam washing onto my beach, the ebb and flow of life's residues seen or felt drifting on lazy horses or contemplative winds. Bits of wreckage, stuff thrown overboard to lighten the ship's load, anything that no longer serves its purpose. Sea creatures and their remnants wash up too. Molluscs, crabs, shells, kelp, the odd fish or bird skeleton, even a whale bone.

I love walking on beaches, the emptier the better. What strange things one finds, spewed from shipping lanes or the ocean depths. Pick one up, turn it over, try to make sense of it. Lift your hand against the sun's glare. What else is scattered on the sand? A thrill rises in your chest. Connections emerge, poetry begins to form. You say to Life, "I want to know you." Life accepts, and so a poem, shyest of all writing, allows itself to be coaxed from shelled creatures and other debris lying there waiting to be discovered. Sometimes word by word, perhaps months or years apart, like the ocean's slow grinding of rock to sand, or all at once in a tidal rush. The poem woos you, lures you into a trance of meaning—secret currents, forgotten places just beyond your grasp. Just … reach … a little … further.

Let's call them bohèmes sometimes, gypsies of the soul. They are children of faith. Like tides, they ebb and flow, a fine balance between reining in and letting go. First, there is the contract. You marry Life; the bohème begins to distil from your swirling passions. As with all relationships, there's only one guarantee: there will be growth if you allow it. For better or worse, you embark on each intoxicating line. For richer or poorer, stanzas arrive in blazes of glory only to be snuffed out when unable to withstand the scrutiny of hindsight. As you brace yourself against birth pangs, you inherit a worthy heir—a vehicle through which your fleeting moments might live on. But just as no child can be expected easily, do not expect bohèmes to be obedient to your flat-earth constraints of what is.

As Wordsworth said, "The Child is father of the Man."

When the bohème is finally born, do not hinder its passage, lest it be starved of air in its most vulnerable moment. Let it scream its rebel life to you. Rejoice, for this moment will never rumble its wheels this way again, nor anywhere in all eternity.

When the pain is over, and your soul is wrung dry, let the bohème sleep. Return occasionally to stroke its cheek. Tweak it here and there, see if it responds with a yawny smile. Find that one word that eludes you. Delight in trepidation as your creation becomes its own self. Discover delicious parallels, concurve double meanings, subtle shades, nuances. Learn from it, the bairn of your soul. Stand in awe and humility: in your smallness, you have consummated beauty, breathed spirit to matter.

Poems are shy exhibitionists. It's taken a long time for me to draw the courage to publish, but at some point, I accepted the truth of the fancy idea I so confidently elucidated: somehow, they really do become their own beings. I hope that this collection brings something like light to your life, that you may refract onward.

Lana Hunneyball
West Sussex, November 2020

Acknowledgements

My family has been incredibly supportive in the many aspects of my windy path. Ants and Fin—loving siblings and *always* there for me. My dad Rod, constant support and Man of Wisdom, and his wife Stella. My two girls, Lou and Kirst: to see how you have overcome your quota of historical and environmental whirlwind is a true inspiration to my own growth. Lastly, my mom Charlotte, who acts selflessly as mentor, not only in life but my writing too. To all of you, thank you. I am me because of you.

Beyond that, and specifically with these poems, talented people have helped me along the road, and I am eternally grateful. Dorian Haarhoff offered valuable feedback, and I tested draft versions of a few at Cape Town's Off The Wall Poetry Performing where I made some of my most enduring friendships. Hugh Hodge and Julia Kramer's couch was always ready for a sleepover and/or a serious debate over coffee or wine—they were like a second family to me in some of my darkest moments. Where would we be without friends? Immense thanks to Jacques Coetzee for editorial input, painstaking assessment, and belief that "I can do it!" Bill Knight, gallant singer songwriter, thank you for your dedicated critical read; Karen Scott and Bonny Sadr for helping process the images; and poet and artist Cathy de Villiers. What's better than spending a Cape winter weekend curled up with hot chocolate and tearing one another's work to shreds? And where would we be without that school teacher who sees the nascent writer and gives us our first thesaurus? I still have the dog-eared thing, and Marion Henderson became a good friend.

Once, at a poetry festival, I paid for half an hour of an established chap's time. He said I should go away and study structure and form. I came away disheartened. Nevertheless, the next day I read one of my poems at a session and got resounding applause. To the lady who ran up afterwards to say I'm a hero—I don't think I am, but thank you. We must believe in ourselves. That doesn't mean not listening to feedback, and it does mean digging deeper than you ever thought you could, but in the end, it's just you and the Godiverse pushing you through that birth canal. Thank you to the many precious friends not mentioned here. They are the cilia that guide us along the fallopian tubes.

And so to that grand and mysterious creative tangible love-force we call God, I'm yours.

<u>Links:</u>

Ants and Fin: teniquatreetops.co.za
Kirsty: www.kirstenhunneyball.co.za
Charlotte: facebook.com/Charlottefkartist
Dorian Haarhoff: dorianhaarhoffblog.co.za
Off The Wall Poetry Performing:
facebook.com/otwpoetry
Jacques Coetzee: jacques.c@mweb.co.za
Bill Knight: facebook.com/Billknightmusic
Cathy de Villiers: facebook.com/cathy.devilliers.54
The grand and mysterious creative tangible love-force
we call God: Close your eyes; breathe; listen.

Flotsam & Jetsam

A half-life of poems

They Say

They say sometimes the precious things
remain so more unsaid.
That, for mere expression's sake
the fibre of a textured love, once uttered
may unthread.

That all unspoken nuances
ingrain upon the soul
growing it, clipping all the unfine bits
to make it whole.

They say that our banalities
are by definitions formed
that words by their nature sell us short
plot against our inner endless
squeezing out precision.

I'll not heed the tempting lure
to keep my thoughts untold
for once released, a frame appears
to shape the void
the womb that births the opus—
esprit undestroyed.

As silence weaves its way
around and in my words
I pray the bellows of our love will press
and breathe blessing to our world.

Precious Dove

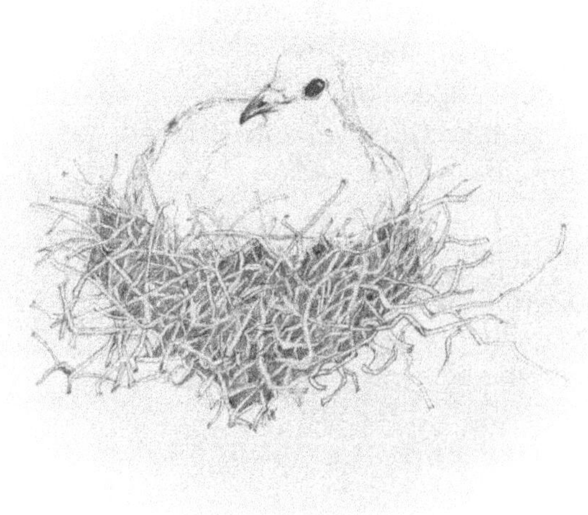

In search of a more precious love
the gentle dove
lifts tired unspent wings
to an open sky, her watchful eye
darts here and there—
perhaps to hitch a ride on an upward burst
of air, that may pass by.

Now and then, the pain of being
just a dove having almost settled in
she sets her wings against the wind to see—
perhaps an accident of fate
might invite a gust towards her ledge
in time to lift the gasping bird to splendoured heights
beyond, beyond.

Could it be, a fall from grace
a wretched trick of circumstance
might close the gap between
never
and take a chance?

She's come to know the wind by now
studied all its temperaments, knows
each pocket of delicious air by name.
From her cleft of unknowingness
she waits.

It's all the dangers there, you see.
A foul and stormy squall
can plunge one's feathered self under wayward streams
lurching towards the sea
down, down
wishing fate had been more kind
and left her
still waiting for this hour.

It's nothingness we fear
yet let it come.
Let irony play me, let me be a tune.
No matter be it melancholy
of lonely flights unflown
no matter't be a precious love
a precious love unknown.

Wildflower

Wildflower, wildflower, set against the sky.
Exquisitely she bursts her very self
upon its canvas deep and blue
strong inside, strong to give
more than till that moment has been lived.

Ah, vanities, her leaves!
Stretching out from root and stem
tenderly, touching their surround
laughing at what storm and caterpillar bring.

Wildflower, wildflower, bent against the wind.
Adversity will come! her shapely stem shouts gaily.
Let us dance as we scatter seeds of loveliness
adorn our heavens and delight
in our sunny blest domain.

Your soul has touched your world—
some see all that they can be
in each petal dressed in awe
and wonder at the treasures yet within.

Wildflower, wildflower, wild as wild can be
how tamed you are by love, you silly thing.
Graciously you bow and humbly grin—
all was folly but to seed this day
when ripe roots tether deeper still
and drink at last their long and aching fill.

Bird of a Feather

Little sparrow on a twine
biding time
biding time
slowly, softly, twist to see
pitter patter, anxious feet

dried-up twigs beneath me.

Rushing to the grocery store
buying more buying more
sadly madly cannot find
(in this turbulence of mind)
where to sit

all the world, and me.

Metamorphosis of Me

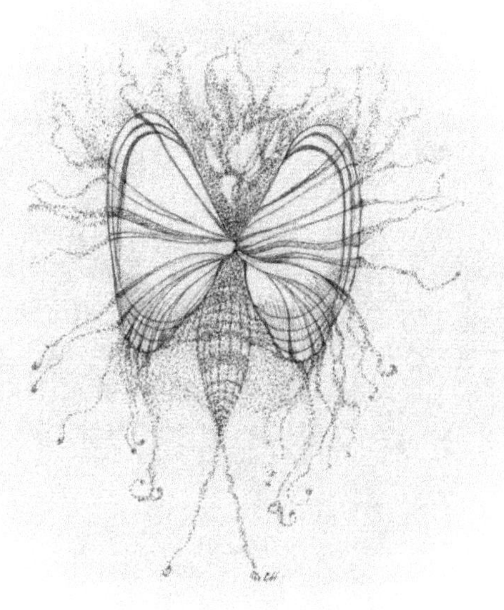

A butterfly
once in caterpillar'd jest
thought to be—something more.
He rode a crest, a splendid wave.
Crashing down, it landed
the bewildered worm
to rest upon the shore.

He shakes his wings—what joy that brings
to shed the crinkled coat
of growing up and wondering
and other childlike things.
No heed or need of leaden legs
but on thrilling wings to soar

how free! To cast off fear
and doubt and pain
and dwelling on what could be.
Forget the lie (there are no wings).
Embrace the now of a zillion stunts and glides
he sings, and celebrates the heady days
of his just reward.

Other 'pillars crouch and wait
knowing for themselves it cannot be.
Who is this monstrous coloured quasi-bird
this unintellectual, this disloyal unlegged inanity
who deems himself at large?

The butterfly soared higher
deaf to all below
became entranced by a bud in a cleft.
Her juicy sap filled his soul with awe.
The promise of togetherness
pulled him up in prospered glee
a distant echo sighing through the crags ...
'more ... more!'

Barren

Barren is the soul that bears no pain.
No birth can hap upon her shores.
She shields no private wisdom
nor thirsts for one accord.

No loss that stares without relief.
No bulging husk cries out for rain.
No salty lips or sun-scorched smiles
no stolen kiss nor unplanned miles
savoured moments, lingered whiles
nor timeless dreams from which to heal.

Just a parched crust stretched towards a scolding sun
shrivelled wasteland
lost in crevices of dread.

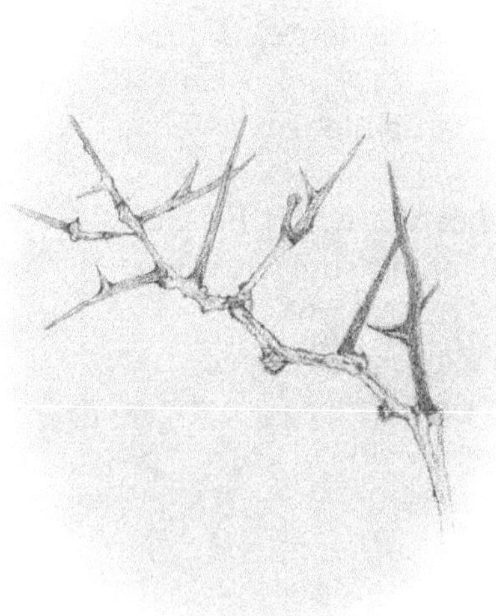

Andante

Wink of Time, you hussy, you all-foreseeing oracle
of mine
fashion queen, selfish teen, old woman
rocking back and forth in convoluted cadence
weaving into memory strands of waning sunlight
and passion run to seed.
In us, enchanted by your spell
your fleeting glimpse
regrets plague, pleasures assuage
gifts of immortal delight wind on
but are gone
each measured beat a compass needle.
You blaze your mark, then
taunt our fickle souls in whirls of infinite latitude
cut short
by the very next breath.

I am but a leaf in the prelude to a violent overture.
Give me strength to hold the weight I seek to flee—
ivories were thrown, but then it was my own
design that caught me, wandering
amidst a slow distending degree
that gathers force in virulence.
Sovereign charge of the pendulum
thrusts its blow.

Devolution

When love grows thin as fine-spun stalactites
a soul's mewling cry.
To touch it, it will break.
When you speak
and no egg-shelled sacrifice
can satisfy the barbed wire mammoth
that roars, thrusting from your mouth
ripping wads of cheek flesh
as it clambers to the floor.

When time laps in lazy taunts
at corpse-scattered beaches.
Past mistakes stretch out before
behind
deadpan
and no mantle-fused nuggets cling to particles of sand
as the tide sucks back last wishes.
Corrugated lips purse
a death rattle in each depleting breath.
Nothing left to buy back youth
or force a smile.

And misjudgements fail
to blossom into morrow's bloom
and sorry hurts too much.
A blood-spattered finger hits the fan
blinding eyes with slashing tongues
and wrong is right or as you will
and true despair is overshot
by a numb and a clamping.

Then do we lose our soul.

To the Lonely

You are heard
in the lashing gale and breeze
searing sun that scorches toughest souls
in the calm embalming warm crisp winter under snow
angry caress of a fickle dream
oceans that mirror our contradictions
churning forth and back from the ever source
in lapping whispers.

If you don't believe me
just listen.

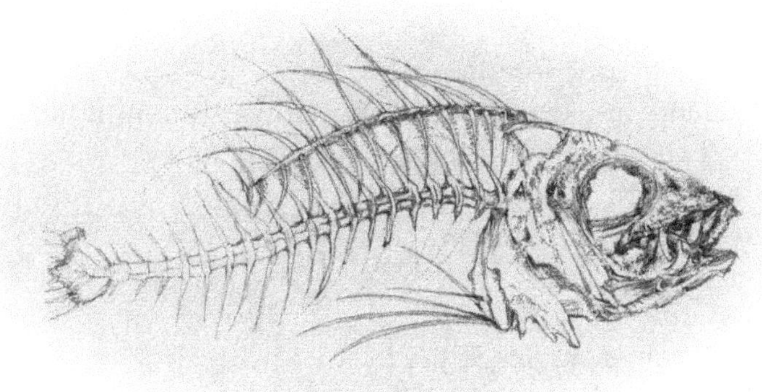

Broken

Born at the stroke of a clock
a split-second choice in a smoke-inhabited shack
urban seepage, masses spread like bacteria.
Life will find a way.

No home to break, it's broken in.
Shut-your-trap-rat-trap
go watch hip-hop on the black and white
but get outta my face!
Broken dreams borrowed from America, never to be got.
We all die, so who cares?
Infinity nags at the culture-fused, subdued residue
of something in me that knows.
But the aphrodisiac acceptance holds me high—
it's my right to be what I wanna be
so I go.

Lull of narcotic freedom then.
Drug-infested disaffected sixties onwards boring cliché
don't care if someone else is getting rich hey—
it's my right.
Give me a bloody break.

Memories of home.
Small hands praying in the mist.
My father who has no hold of heaven—
hello? I'm going insane.
Your time will come
your ill be done
through everything and everyone you touch
as it is around you, everywhere.

Don't break the furniture, alcohol is better than bread.
Forgive me for being born
as Others have been born against me.

Now these three things abide:
Money, Greed and Power.
But the greatest of these is loneliness—
a broken heart can always blame
deaf to the mating call of time.

This, then, is how I learn what God is:
most conditional love.
Conditioned to forget what we always knew:
dry crumbs and grape juice can't fix when you're broke.
Can't buy you a girlfriend.

So I grab my stick or my gun and my lack and my lost
and break in—
to the inside places where it's empty and cold
where I need so much to be me.

Breaking news: Youths held for smash and grab
valuables removed
heads down, hands cuffed
shuffle in to face the glare:
You contravened the jungle law.
Your sentence is life
manacled to the chasm
where the gavel falls.

The beast is broken
subdued sub judice sub-standard.
The spirit's but a shadow. We are safe.

Fiddling the books
while home burns

New Brighton[1] burns brightly
splendid and laden with passion
fused in tempered unity—
humble fragile tin and scalded faces.
A reprisal of blistering sores sears and toils
at the high life, wine, women and song
as Rainbow Nation ablutes the palette
of a demented artist
whose private angst plays out
amongst the hum.

Paraffin-incensed tempo drifts
a slow winding spiral, wisp of Africa time
proceeds against the brazen sky.
A silhouette of far-off mountains
splays itself to the coming night.
The heat, the beat, the need to eat.
The wait, the hate, the hovel crate
unbearable hue, sting of an age
lost in a haze, till tomorrow.
We wait.

Somewhere, a cop takes a bribe
in an obscure backroad, bepebbled, aflame.
Officials sleep like babes
books balanced, unchallenged, plotting the course—
fear driven impasse to the Promised Land.

Peacetime

The jagged edge of peace cuts deep
twists its stiletto heel
into the wound of the forgotten soldier
then twists again.
For certain, it was his last summer
lying half rotted already, cold pain sweating
alone
but for the hope his death might bring.

Still Life

Two, previously young, too long ago
bicker about ... shoelaces?
Two half-lives half lived in semi-paralytic symbiosis:
a dream.

No great passion to tell.
Skeletons in cupboards sit, heaps of anorexic dust
disintegrated two score dry squalls and two still lives ago.
Daily appetites are met: one low fat protein, three veg.
One small glass of wine.
He, arranged at one end of the matrimonial chequerboard
contemplates his secret sin:
a chocolate bar, unprescribed for his condition
hidden also.
She stares at her quarry, half pitying, half remembering.

No great crime to tell, except of these two lives
a watery affront to history's sacrifice:
battlefields of loins that fell
or not, to the rack-a-tack-tack of fate's roulette wheel.

Rack-a-tack-attack shoelaces.
Bitter insults fall on angry spittle.
Calm reigns once more.
He disappears through the back door
to fiddle in a box of tools

shoelaces ... dragging ... still
on the cold kitchen floor.

Pie

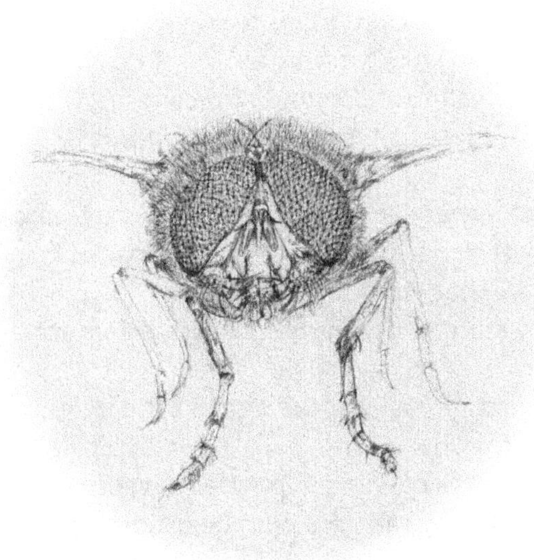

Everyone's got
their piece of the pie
throwing their hands up and screaming
OH WHY?
Stuck like flies to its sugary crust
waiting and waiting
to turn back to dust.

Barking Dogs

There's an iron mist settled on the hearts of now
a cold self-pity mocked up as fear.
And fear itself hounds that trail
pursues our calloused shame into caverns
where deaf mutes sit in awe of symphonies.

I saw a babe that ere it could be born was found
a fossil, soft bones etched into fragile rock.
I cried tears that would not come.
Their salty sting will never sate my dried-up tongue.

Dogs howl at ghosts packed against the walls.
They long to run
ancient lineages bawling in padded unison along the tar
but are denied by masters who hear nothing
ever
save their own stomachs rumbling
day after day after day and night
injustice throws its hammers against their ears
but they will not move.
Feet set firmly in the stones they throw.
Them. Us.
They who suffer.
We who nod in disapproval when a child is born
in a drain
its innocence sucked down with our excuses.

Dumb mockery, democracy.
Your afterbirth attracts the flies
and you are a far cry
licking self-inflicted wounds with reproachful eye.
Oh, that you were born to a mother, a father
who willed your closeting against the chill.
Indifference turns your lips to blue.

Yet may it be, when the dogs stop barking
day after day after day and night
your time will come.

Free Man

Look at us, your hands.
From rock and sweat we hewed a nation
that could not love.
That gorged us to the very pistol edge of sanity.
Then, crimson chafed and scarred, you held us high
and we clapped freedom songs
till every calloused drop fused a tear of joy.

But now! You fling us into pockets lined with guilt
and shrug.
You set your jaw and hood your eyes
like a sly dog.
Are you not proud of your victory
tithed from the ancestors' gift
soft flesh thrust onto hard steel in secret places
for the freeing of our manacles?

Or was all that a lie?

You throw a bottle down your throat
then ram it in your sister, your mother, your brother—
anyone who will not be
obedient, as are we
who see the terror in their eyes and shake with shame
at what we have become.
Oh, Master, please, we beg you—free us
from the power
you have stolen
like a coward
from the weak.

If we could ask a moment's rest
we'd pray: let us build with the rocks we throw.
Let the pain-carved hands of the boy we know
lift children up on shoulders, high
to see the monster in defeat, dreams
stitched new from the ash white remnants of our minds
by us—your hands—and those who
loosed at once from your tyrant's grip
would love you.

I Remember

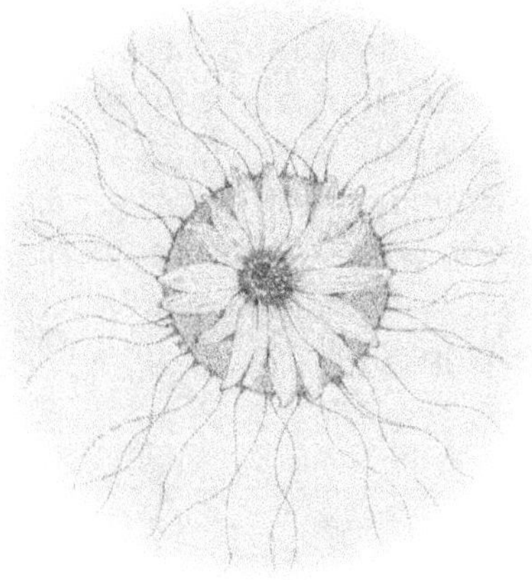

That one once you were real
but not the world.
Your hand lay next to the empty cup.
I floated in a surreal dream
but it was real, your hand. I could simply have
shifted
a tiny bit
then, calloused and hewn with vitreous time
the soft under-flesh of yours
would have been on mine and
but I didn't.
The coffee shop was full of people
and my life with reality
where dreams push in like climate change
unwanted, unstoppable, overwhelming
and things can never be the same.

Ode to the shade of the tree

Is this it? Is it now?
When one universe of love and furrowed brow
having squeezed itself through one medium-sized pot
of steaming adolescence—sifted, milled and tossed—
bumping frenzied molecules against
everything it can
stops.
Asks: Is this it? Is it now?
Do I say
fuck it. I did my best.
I concede.
If this world wins
and even should my own passions return
before they run to seed

I did the very best I could.

Polity

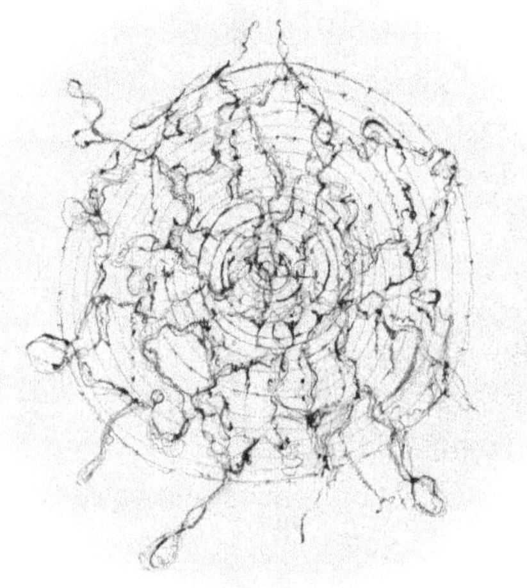

Let's take a trip through the eye of just one storm.
A boy on a bed, squarely made, in a dorm.
He stares out at trees, safe from the mayhem
then at the door, the system that made him.
A mother will never bring cookies through there
but when he steps out, brave as a bear
he must carry the world as many like him
born as a leaf, on a breeze, on a whim.

An idea, long ago—the Greeks made an atom
the root of all matter, vast spaces within them.
Colliding like marbles, never at rest
infinite frenzy, unyielding yet pressed
with such vigour by that unstoppable force
into life so fragile it must take its course.
No choice but to be the form that's assumed
no matter what storms beyond branches may loom.

A word, long ago—polis—city state
changed the axis around which nations rotate.
The curious idea we can live without death
tip our hat to our neighbour and let go the rest.
In dreams we might tame beasts within and without
not beat with our fists but discuss—be polite.
Our atoms may seek and never be still
yet we might put to dance the thug who would kill.

Outside, storm trees shake with a murderous rage
as the wild unmothered comes of age.
Never made to say 'sir' or hold back a plate
with love, respect for his inner state.
He stands, and his soul shifts away from the bed
from which all ripples go, gaining power as they spread
to the polis, the city, the heresy of words
his atoms pierce on, force their will to be heard.

When he dines with disaster as a businessman
cold eyes calculating the most expedient plan
will he wonder what innocence may yet dodge his spear
what wars by a gesture, a smile, a just ear?
But violence quakes amid continents locked
in the Self that is new on the primal block.
It's a question to ask, always has been
can one choose, even then, look away, to the dream?

Word

Once upon a deep breath, one exquisite inhalation
and then upon the fair wind of satisfied release
there chanced upon a thought upon a life so fleeting
through the finite tenderness of one moment in repose:
a word.

Couched in half an eggshell
afloat a sea of air
its tiny canvas groans, bucks and duels
the unkind swells of its forbears' mounting wit.
Walls of jade stare dry-eyed down, and then—
oh mercy, mutiny within.
The vessel's hurled, china cup against tyrant's fist
but holds strong
between intention and the fair listener's ear

waiting, as a lover's not been met
a child's frantic search in a sea of hands
a soul waking to life's fragile call—
that single thread of which sanity's composed.

See there, a lighthouse casts its faithful glow
lest the word founder on rocks jagged from antiquity.
It bears down for one last push
bolstered by what's unspokenly agreed.
Eyes catch in fishing nets. Land ahoy!
This frail boat's weathered doldrums
that suck wind like a gossiper's tongue
braved the force of its own heart's vortex
and found shade against the sun.

Now, and with a sigh, it docks
berths the silky folds of a synapsed pledge
and the next moment is born.

Visitor's Lament

My heart is lost in Scotland
not sure where exactly.
A hundred white horses charged right through—
strange, I must have looked up then.
Would I find it, if I could, in the simple blue
of far hills' fine-drawn splendour
languishing behind silent taunts—you will miss us so!
Did the boundless lochs steal it to their depths
as I breathed them in?
Or did the deep damp earth suck me down
through feet of thousands gone before
in glens and braes where green fern tendrils twist
in a temptress dance
and each speckled stone is a place to hear the soul.

Perhaps it's lost to swirling mists and welkin sighs
that churn me in their witch's brew
interspersed with promises
nymphs frolicking on shafts of light, this sky
that's witnessed all from ancient Pict to Tory
wept aeons with each axe that fell
across the centuries, shouted up their story
through every battle trod, every faithful clod
of earth
as a loving hand, as a fragrant whisper.

This is where I remember
the things I do not know.

Yet, will I go.
At once pulled from and reunited with myself.
May I be as sturdy as this mad old land
sow its seeds in places that I go
all be my step much lighter now.
Aye, it is so.
If I could devise which moment stole from me
this tired heart
perhaps I'd think to leave it there
with one promise: to return.

Burial Ground

You sailed away in an unmarked grave
a flailing speck on history's wave
back across that sea.
I saw you, invisible, brave
your every breath
precious to me
poison cross, grit steel grin and a flag
flying high with the soul you gave
to join the ranks:

– – – HIV – – –

Rank and defiled, forgotten remnants
of a discarded age
cheeks smooth as ancient thorns
that impis[2] trod
blood dripping for their nation.
Who listen, even now, through the ancestors' wind
tears slow as stalactites
hands cracked from salty drips
holding on with bitter pride
in a dream, marching 'cross the plains
assegais thrust to the sky, leathered feet a-dance
stampeding drought-hard bushes that scatter the graves
that ebb you away
on that cold blood sea.

Shards of starlight slice your faces—
but your faces!
They shine through the fog of collective forgettery.
I smile, lifting my hand, but you're all caught up as one
hauling your strength from under the magnet of death.
Holocaust-thin ribcages rise, brandishing decrepit arms
claiming blade by retching blade
the nubs of our humanity.

All this, I tell you, I see
but really
I just wish you were here
with me.

Marimba Band

People watch, arms folded, or they stop pushing prams.
One man holds a hand to his chin.
Our rhythms begin.
We strike down with force, then lift
releasing joyful leaf-fulls of spring
strike, bite down, release, searing beauty from the deep
under our sticks, deep in the mines of our waterless souls
where we drown because it's too far
too far down here.
Again we strike, thumping down in unison
harmony deep
pushing up from under the lives we're in.
My mouth cracks, panting lava
the music rises through me
around me.
It is me!
Love breaks through my prism
out over people's heads, raining down confetti
like a wedding from the sky.

I'm so happy!
Sweat pours as I work the bars, beat them and beat them
till I burst with pride.
Ouboet,[3] the tall one behind—
a panga[4] scar marks his face
pushes and squeezes his dark oily cheek.
His mouth can't stop smiling too.

We are free!

How I wish my chaos had been mastered
before I was shattered by the knuckle-hate of life.
Clash, thwack, crunch, splatter
afterthought of cruel disorder kept in play
pitter-patter
here came little feet with no rhythm
slaves to fickle winds.

We're nearly done.
Our feet dance with our arms like puppets
and we forget the people's eyes.
Free from the shackles of our dust, it rises
blending with our uniforms.
One shifty-eyed warden moves his feet closer.
The back of his hand holds the air above his knobkerrie.[5]
The others suck in their bellies.
Dust floats out and settles, fine grains on sunburnt faces.
People nod and start to walk
minus their five rand that sits in the kettle
for us to collect.

Before we go back.

Valediction

It didn't work, or so they say.
We, or I, failed to mash our boxes into lives to be filled
ticked and nodded at with safety-net satisfaction.
Oh, the desperate urgency required of our equations.
So, why then? Too much clanging from the Big Machine?
The squash box, expectation?
Propriety and madmen, tribal gangs swarming
the corridors of our minds
hunting outposts of poetry and sun
blasting our deepest undiscovered passions
in great globs of flesh and blood against the Wall?

Or did we simply meet as A and B
and part as 14.11 and a wobbly zee?

It didn't work.
But do they see the souls we have become?
The deep-grained much of who we are
now that our splattered wall is a canvas
and our souls free from nodding eyes?
That our hurting is a seed.
May you find the love that draws you deeply
brings you to yourself
makes you want to dance, for it wasn't me.
And may we be forgiven our stubborn frailty
that neon blinking blanking-out zen-ophobia of our age
and be still.

Ancient wisdom awaits our birth.

Storm Waiting

The weeds on these gravel-strewn graves
eke past dry soil to sun
and a few drops of rain.
Chiselled letters, one fading with each century
weep from tilting headstones.
Below, unremembered souls let ants tickle their tummies
as they wait for us.
You are a sudden birth
bleaching my soul across this rich arid Karoo[6]
and all that's buried in me.
I was willing to trade it for a few pregnant beads
flopping down in a merciless tease
now here's the flood, pushing me back
dragging my legs—
the undertow uproots my parched aeolian crust
that, until moments ago
was grindingly, faithfully, dying.
Can my particles hold?
Will you crave the chaos of the storms that sent you
and leave me birthed but helpless?
Any port, next open door, next aimless track
as you heave your load across the grave
tickling its tummy, oblivious to the soul below?

Do you care?
ask the daisies that dance among the weeds
whispering soft yellow promises to hot stones
and the sky.

Balloon Ride

Together alone, floating on candy floss pink
and flamingos laughing
between eros and logos, subtlety and fear of loss
we flow and fly, live and die
dip, sway and jab at circumstance
with our love's feather.

Light breaks through from above and below. So it goes.
The last dance, bequeathed to us
eros and logos, dipping and sway
close your eyes, love, believe.
Let me swallow your soul with my kisses.

Can I stay? Suspended here with you?
Is it arrogance, this decrying of the low
the rude? Conversations about lineage
quaffing and coiffeur
and coughing to clear the circular track.
Who'll win this time peeping over the wine glass rim?

Endless voices! Sucked into the vortex, la-di-race-course
discourse, never forward, never down, never deep
only sometimes—fleeting smiles, a dip of the toe
a shrieking shrink
a scurry back to the Cage, the Cave
nip-tucked safety of the soul's slave.

And it's OK.

Together alone, tinkling chatter floats away
candy floss pink
flamingos laughing
eros, logos
flow, fly, dip, sway.
Close your eyes, love
sshhhhh.

Alchemy

We will have a gentle house
where souls wear soft socks
and roam free of the dust of their assaulted selves
and bookcase shelves invite to wayward journeys
and conversations escape like nymphs
on uncorked champagne bubbles
cosseted by the well-worn arms
of our faded leather settee.

Outside, the storm clouds of our younger selves
may gather with respect
and nourish our wild garden.
At the threshold, anguish surrenders its vile breath
repelled by our love's force that bars defeat
of self through other
while we make love at the fireplace.

Who or what spark-short comet tail dares
invade our paint-splattered
love-cluttered light-drenched haven
other than it be vanquished as it strikes our atmosphere
exploding into nothing
a refracting speck in the kaleidoscope
transmuting our skies?

Eudaimonia

Strange peace, this, descends, an attack
of the soft peach creamy sleep dream
a moment, cushioned
a crystal enclaved in the gentlest womb
that against jagged circumstance protects.
A look from you, or walking.
A cerise geranium catching the light—just so
or sitting forward, lost in a book, a thought.
Peace intervenes, uninvited.
As unfamiliar as a knock, a falling of the chest
a shake of the head, a half closing of the door
then sudden recognition of an old friend.

Exact relief. Carved up against
the stubborn habits of all our discontents
it comes.

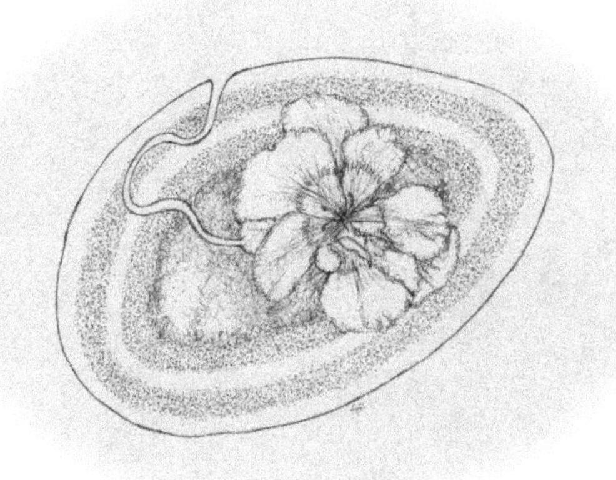

Geomorphology

Illusion dies.
Hearts break.
Rivers run
and mountains shift their course
so slow
grinding grand bravado
and that persistent barnacle, hope
into sand to beach the soul.
If only (my love) you had asked
what lay below, but wandered
beyond the mantle
pressing rotted leaves to diamond
and even then, to magma coursing, yearning
for a chink in the crust
a head for its heat, primal release—
souls catch sight across cool, damp mist—
had you not been content
tending your many rods
hanging from the edge
I would have told you.

But I forget.
Illusion is dead.

Be Longing

I was Somebody once.
The ring said so.
Belonged, belonged to, was taken, taken up, taken in
absorbed, consumed, contained.
Digested
like a buck in a crocodile's stomach
stops flailing, resigns itself
to belonging.

Now, I'm Nobody. I stare at four walls
at all my four-square loss.
Truth doesn't pay the bills
and nobody calls.
Was it I who held up the facing mirrors
the infinite illusion of Self through Other
hunting down the severed connection
private poster child for the vacuum-sponge-crack-addict
of our interminable wanting?

I'm nobody now, nobody that I was.

Hickory Dickory Docked

You stay, wound up, wounded as a glued-up clock
a fat bloodied tick stuck in your forgetting gong—
that capricious apron skirt of maternal affliction.
You cannot bestir yourself a second forward
or turn, and see that once you were behind
in a place that bears remembering
a mulling over with mulled wine
and a rueful grin.

Don't you ache to feel the wind
in those limp-angled arms
that clog the passage to wondrous now?
My life, and Life, it wants
it wants to dance, cheek tucked in under your laughing face
the thrill of your deep brass chime
and the tinkling brook of my heart
fretful layered thing stifled in geology
that it is.

What perfection do they think they can bring
to this world
with nothing but glib glued sketches
air drawings
ephemeral fumblings
desperate to be had and to be held
fondled and laughed with
in the greyed-out spaces
before our splitting second is gone?

Insomnia

Hormones, bedbugs, church-bells
and the fickle Muse
send buzzed-up tendons of a searching heart
on vampire stakes to the surface—
meek milk, cheap Chinese reality
far from cauldrons breezing the surgeon's knife
where craving souls carve themselves away in soapstone ...
the slippery eel of the hi-jacked I
soars above the bells
the dredge of lumps and bugs and bills
calling from month-end instead of Her—
thundering Pegasus, hoof and wing.

When we seek death
is it the pristine crimson-buttered edge
from which the urge to slip?
Unconditional saturate
clinched cliché of warm wet womb
nail-hard slicing out of dogged desire
and endless sirens.

Yet, God gave us silence.
Each tear's plea on bird-shot nerves.
Anxiety of affluence (no crops to tend)
shoots us back again
down to peace
and the cock crows.

Hubris

Oh, how the ladies sit like tight brooding hens
clutching their quivering labia at the … of your words.[7]
Clamouring clams a-chorusing all, amen, ah, oh!
As your beard tips forth beneficence in quanta
light-sized food stamps
to the one-by-one of their desperate queue.
By osmosis they're touching your hem
nay, the crumbs dispensed by your next 'ahem.'
When you speak, so it is, to the seething plebeian Them
Amen.
Angelic choirs annunciate your next stanza
coiffed by the nose hairs of their fairer state.

Down boy. Through the fetid, nit infested layers—
chickenshit bullshit seeping through
the mouldy, stodge-damp mattress, that
'do you know who I am?' glance across watering eyes:
the dark daunted fears of your hubris.

Take a dive.
There's more poetry in the pinkie of the klonkie[8]
on the street corner
banging out his molecules and his story
against old goat skin stretched across a rusty paint tin
singing with his teeth that lack the strength to bite
even one mark down on his time—but are smiling—
than in you.

But oh god!
How the mountains bow to your encryptions.
How thesaurus titillates and fibrillates as you ruminate
and cogitate your high-minded metaphors
that only you can see
from the phallus of your fallacies—
the plague and lie of your primacy.

Sorry, do go on.
Hold your nose though.
Pinch it back against the stick-thin
stink of your platitudes.
Go—find your shrivelled pea—that moment
when your princess soul awoke your muse
cracked it open, found its true onion
that voluptuous fruit
and heard!
Before the mighty mythy scythe
the vanguard of your high priesthood
ran up the steeply spire
and the high clear bell (your mind, see)
cleaved your heart in two.

Scarborough Beach

If your heart breaks
and time stands still
find yourself a spot
above a lower hill
and watch the morning shadow
caress the trees as light engulfs
it, hear it beat
with slow remembering, a lull
its fluttering plight
distant now
free as a paper gull.

Inventory

How much?
yells I into the void.
How much longer, harder, more?
In how many milk-and-horn-prodded dreams
can the sinewed sailor tether the ocean to his boat?
Which infinity must be hounded, parried to the craw
till it finds its one lost thing
deep under quivering ice-picked thaw?

How many acorns will fill a begging bowl?

Or less perhaps, all the more
smidgeon pigeon peck, nail-scrape of open sky
tattered flap of weathered sail
teaspoon of sea, muted roar
silent swallowed word?

Just enough, whispers the voice
to hold the door.

Binary

We're embedded, you and I
our codes locked.
Zeroes, all the days before we met
ones for when we had.
Zero before you entered me
your thorn, one, and all the wounding seconds
I miss you when you're gone.
Our mouths, our tongues, our eyes
their coded looks
locked in spiral unity
open hands that know
and feel, with satellite precision
our desire arabesque across the milky sky
breasts compressed, a singularity.
A compass and itself
an apple on a shelf
an other and itself—falling
piercing space with laughter
its floating one to our wisp-thin nil
expanding, unbounded, our love.

Oh, but zero for the times you never heard
my voice, a soundless gong.
One for the slamming door, its ricochet
wrestling marshmallow on impotent hinge.
Empty, my heart, swamp-drained
in the wake of your rage
as it plundered murderously on and on.

Zip for mouths and ears that couldn't
and for the scores we kept.
Ones for all the sleepless nights
I wept and wept.

Nought for these walls.
One for the one who was left
and my phone, its silent dignity.
Zero my sadness, your empty folded into me
(flesh-eating bacteria)
but here I stand

one, with two cupped hands.
You are free.

Fountain of Use

Desire, unbridled, came
mistook for wanting
and your Arctic core, its desperate maw
found wanting.
Only so many hairline cracks in ancient porcelain jars
can collect your pain
before exploding
too fragile for your idle bone
(desert heat sucked its marrow long ago).
They lie too
beside their emptied selves
in tiny ivoried boxes fashioned with authority
for their harried particles
desiccated but for this short burst:
pleasure mistaken for Life.
Desire pressed to the edge
where ice shatters if it does not melt.

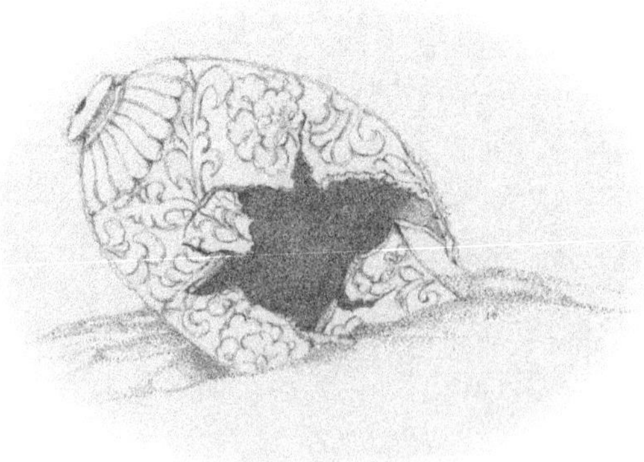

Seduction

We're very similar, you and I
I'm still figuring things out
you're better off without me, I have too much baggage
(commitmentphobe)
((can't seem to keep it in my pants))
(((affirmation junkie, mommy/daddy/colonial baggage)))
(((((Fear of Rejection)))))
My steering wheel flew off, you see
knocked out solar systems
plus, they took away farming.
Not now, never was, never will be my fault.
Oh god, it is me isn't it? Beat me, then
I'm petrified of getting old, dying alone …
but then again, carpe diem.
I'm programmed, don't you know, to seminate
(the Male Project is in Crisis)
((Can't think past my dummy))
Waaaah!
(((((Mother, mother let me return through the wound I made
—before you speared my puckered need)))))
But hey …
why worry about stuff that may never happen—
right?
It's all ego anyway. Stand back. Observe. Live in the now.

(Actually, it's all just too much effort
but thanks, really, for the screw).

Whiskey Devil

I'll call you now and then
my tinder-box friend.
You'll twirl me in your arms, your hands, and then
he promised with his body (you understand)
my one-night stand
you'll gently blow my tumbleweeds
my just-deserted landscape
will unfreeze
        time slips in again
liquid love
one-step, two-step, three-step swirl
  (tip of the cap for each)
music of the fears plays again
the old standards, familiar jazz—
wash (out) repeat—
but for this moment, you're all that.
Neither frenemy nor end, just an ancient postmark
on the fray
one fine needle in the romping hay
(it really – will – all – be – okay).

I'll call you, alright
but until I do, you'll be a gentleman
and stay.

Radio Silence

Not that nothing needs to be said
but is my silence loud enough?

Alright, listen. I'm shooting out static.
I'm a porcupine shooting out quills
huddled in a ball, arrows limp against the void.

Retreat. It's the only trick.
Waves assault the senses
through the eyes, through the ears, it's those
bedevilled rainbows we hear.
Through fingertips we invite them in—
images to taunt our helplessness.
The point of the thrill
is the point of a drill
a thousand bullet pins to the skull
as we flick and toss
between wanting to be free
AND WANTING TO BE TOLD.
Am I one, are we one
or has our great calamity only just begun?

Maybe I'll call tomorrow
find the frequency.
Don't take it personally. I just—can't—take
the noise.

Flower

After time, cosmos yielded to wind, and she was born.
Break! said Life to the incumbent seed
for I crave to be a flower
to flow, carry you to Love's fecundity.

So she pushed and broke, absorbed Life's greedy gifts
and when there was pain, broke again, turned green
then, cutin tearing, yearned with bloody-minded moxie
broke and found the sun.

Was pushed again, stretched and borne to bud
cried, When will we be
this bloom you crave?
My years rise in pillars of salt
and dread like hot tar
as I hunger for your bloom.

Then burst! said Life to the incumbent bud
Release the shell that is too hard
the stem that will not bend
the shoe that does not fit
the mind that will not grow
the ear that cannot hear
the bud that is too small
the chrysalis that does not serve
the love that is not Love—
let us flow!

And when our bloom is done
fall to seed again
for there is no end
to flower.

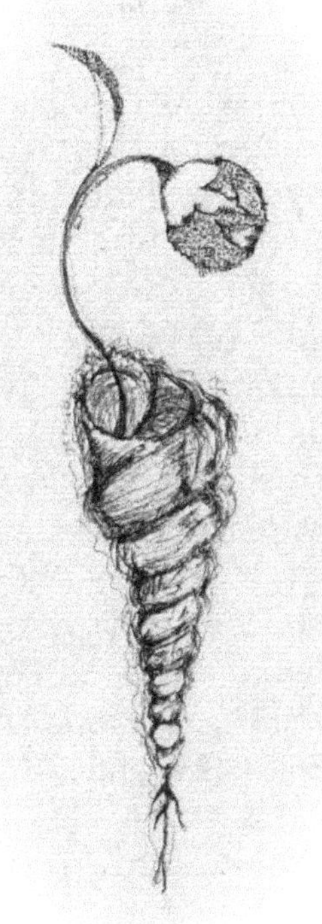

About the Author

Lana Hunneyball

Lana was born in Pretoria, South Africa and grew up in Johannesburg. She studied a BA at the University of Cape Town, majoring in English and Psychology.

As a young mother of two daughters, she pursued many endeavours, including working as a clown, to avoid climbing onto the corporate hamster wheel.

In 1997 she started her own business designing and illustrating workplace communication and training materials, servicing many industries – mainly in Port Elizabeth, South Africa. She designed courses on HIV/AIDS and Integrity and Diversity amongst many other projects and was actively involved in community work. She was a founding member of a Trust for HIV affected children and co-founder of noPEnuke, a community group that raised awareness around the proposed building of a nuclear power plant near Port Elizabeth.

She has always had a love affair with words. In 2017 she completed an Honours degree in English Studies (part-time) through UNISA. She has a CMP Diploma in Proofreading and Editing Level 4.

In 2018 she moved from South Africa to the UK to work as a live-in carer (care-giver) and forge a path as a writer. Flotsam and Jetsam is her first published work.

EMAIL: lana@lanahunneyball.com
lanahunneyball@gmail.com
FACEBOOK: facebook.com/lanahunney
INSTAGRAM: @lanahunneyball
WEBSITE: lanahunneyball.com

Endnotes

<u>1. Page 14:</u>
New Brighton (English)

Under Apartheid, New Brighton became "the first officially black [segregated] residential area in the greater Port Elizabeth [now Gqeberha] area."[1] Unfortunately, like many so-called 'townships', the social problems associated with poverty, corruption, and bad governance persisted post-1994.

"Many of Athol Fugard's plays are set in New Brighton."[2] Fugard felt inseparable from Port Elizabeth, and it inspired much of his work.[3]

Living in this part of the Eastern Cape, South Africa for nearly thirty years gave me unique insight into the exquisite discomfort its physical and spiritual desolation can bring to a seeking artist's heart. I would regularly escape to the dusty hamlet of Nieu Bethesda (where he set his play "The Road to Mecca") to write, and stayed in one of Fugard's houses there for a stint. He is one of my fundamental literary influences.

<u>2. Page 30:</u>
Impis (Nguni)

Historically, *impis* were Zulu warriors, known best for their role under the Zulu king, Shaka (c. 1787 – 1828). "*Impi* is a Nguni word meaning war or combat and by association any body of men gathered for war,"[4] and so the word has broadened to denote "a body of Zulu warriors or other southern African native armed men."[5]

<u>3. Page 32:</u>
Ouboet (Afrikaans)

Ouboet is a broadly used endearment or first name meaning "older brother or a male friend."[6]

4. **Panga** (Nguni)

"A large, broad-bladed African knife used as a weapon or as an implement for cutting heavy jungle growth, sugarcane, etc.; machete."[7]

<u>5. Page 33:</u>
Knobkerrie (Afrikaans and Khoekhoe)

A wooden stick with a knob at the end. "The name derives from the Afrikaans word *knop*, meaning knob or ball and the Khoekhoe or San word *kirri*, meaning walking stick." Called an *iwisa* in traditional Zulu culture, a *knobkerrie* was generally used for chasing off animals and as a "swagger stick, ceremonial object, or even as [a] snuff container." In modern times, the *knobkerrie* has gained symbolism not only as a traditional weapon but also as a signifier of peace (through being laid down).[8]

<u>6. Page 35:</u>
Karoo (Afrikaans, borrowed from Khoekhoe)

"A semi-desert natural region of South Africa … the Karoo is partly defined by its topography, geology and climate, and above all, its low rainfall, arid air, cloudless skies, and extremes of heat and cold."[9]

Driving through the Karoo Basin, you're at the bottom of an ancient shallow sea, now barren scrub dotted by flat-topped mountains, *kopjes* (small hills) and rocky outcrops. In its bosom, sediments deposited eons ago hold invaluable fossil records of Earth's geological past. Its rugged majesty takes your breath away.

<u>7. Page 44:</u>

In line 2 of "Hubris" you'll find a set of ellipses. This is the reader's (or performer's) invitation to inhale and then exhale with all the might and pomposity they can muster.

<u>8. **Klonkie** (Afrikaans)</u>

Technically a derogatory word for a 'coloured' person in South Africa, it is derived from the "diminutive blend of *klein* ('small') + *jong* ('boy')."[10]

However, as with so many raw nuances of human experience, there are layers. Firstly, 'coloured' is not seen as pejorative in South Africa. This may, of course, change as language and culture evolve. Mixed race people in South Africa are, historically, protective of this term as they see themselves as distinct from 'white' or 'black'. This, in turn, is a function of deeply ingrained race thinking. Thereby hangs a thesis.

As for *klonkie*, its meaning here can be read in two ways. Firstly, as the speaker's projection of the arrogant perspective of the subject of the poem and, secondly, in a more innocent way. Growing up as a white person in South Africa, it was quite normal to call young 'coloured' kids *klonkies*. It was just a word. That doesn't make it right, but we must be careful not to strip the soul and history from our languages. In this poem, therefore, it also points to the innocence and systemic powerlessness of the most vulnerable children.

As for poetry, it is meant to be paragrammatic, meaning the deliberate and creative use of linguistic devices such as wordplay, double meanings, puns, and alterations to introduce multiple layers of interpretation. Enriching a poem's complexity invites readers to explore deeper dimensions of meaning and significance.

1. https://en.wikipedia.org/wiki/New_Brighton,_Eastern_Cape
2. https://en.wikipedia.org/wiki/New_Brighton,_Eastern_Cape
3. https://files.eric.ed.gov/fulltext/ED374475.pdf
4. https://en.wikipedia.org/wiki/Impi
5. https://www.merriam-webster.com/dictionary/impi
6. https://en.wiktionary.org/wiki/ouboet
7. https://www.dictionary.com/browse/panga
8. https://en.wikipedia.org/wiki/Knobkerrie
9. https://en.wikipedia.org/wiki/Karoo
10. https://en.wiktionary.org/wiki/klonkie

Notes ...

Use these pages ... doodle ... play ... jot down your thoughts ...

Close your eyes ... let go ... let be ...

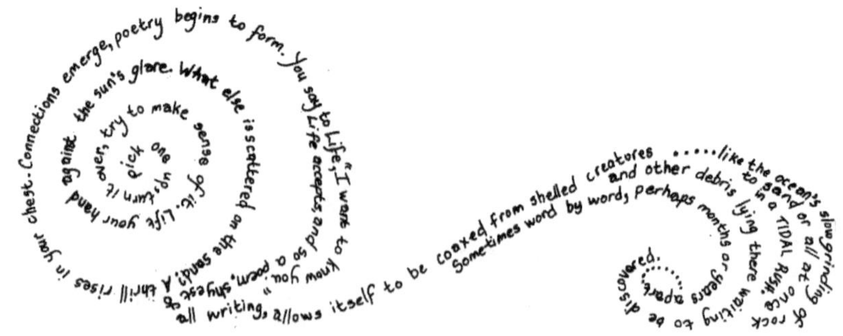

A universe of purpose awaits a listening heart ...

...As with all relationships, there is only one guarantee: there will be growth if you allow It. For better or worse, you embark on each intoxicating line for richer or poorer, stanzas as they arrive in blazes of glory only to be snuffed out, and then unable to withstand the scrutiny of hindsight...

Everything is speaking ...

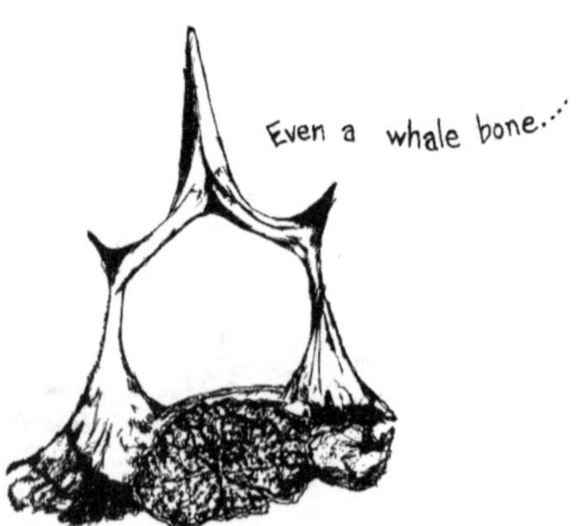

Inspiration is breath ... open your heart ...

Breathe ... spirit to matter ...

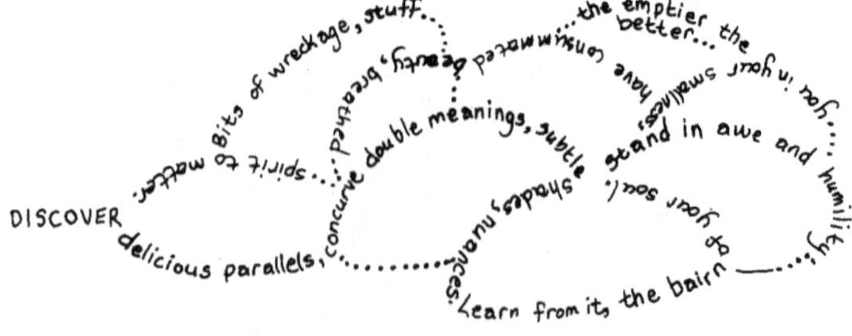

www.ingramcontent.com/pod-product-compliance
Lightning Source LLC
Chambersburg PA
CBHW061431050726
47593CB00006B/2313